AF608993

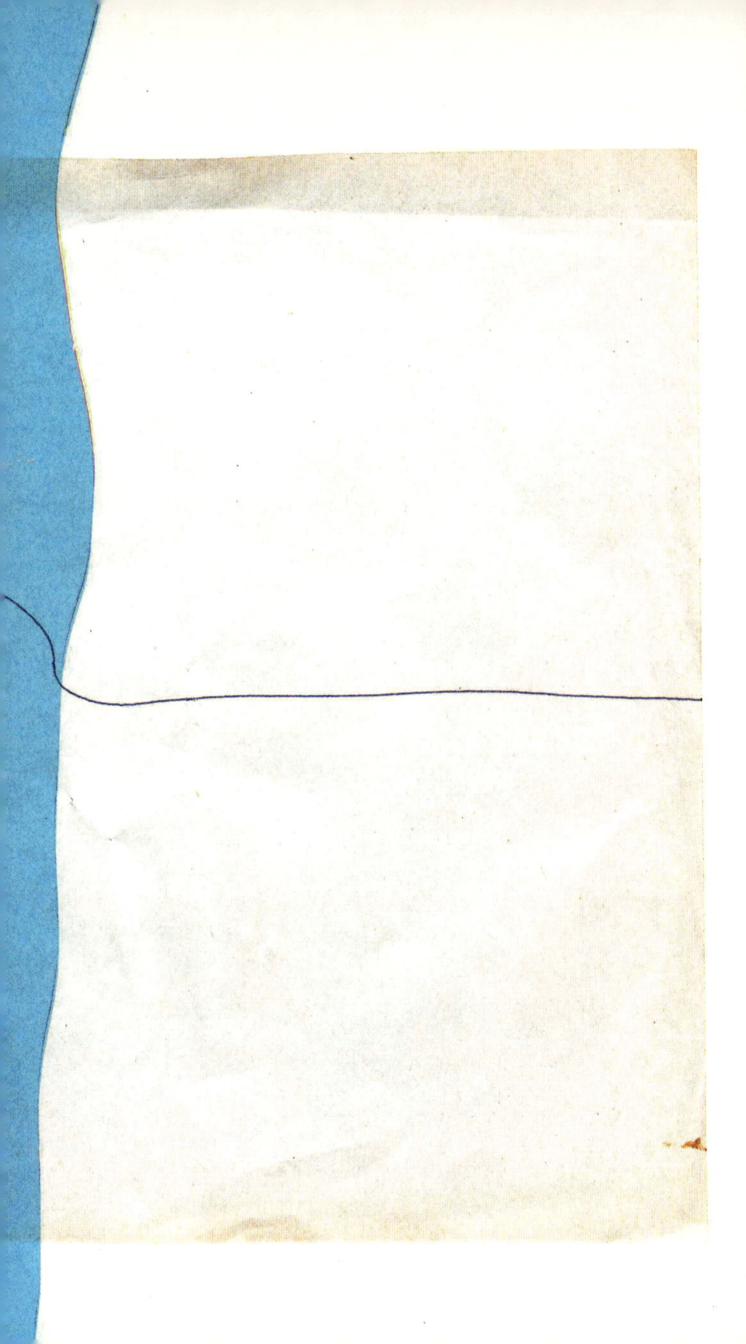

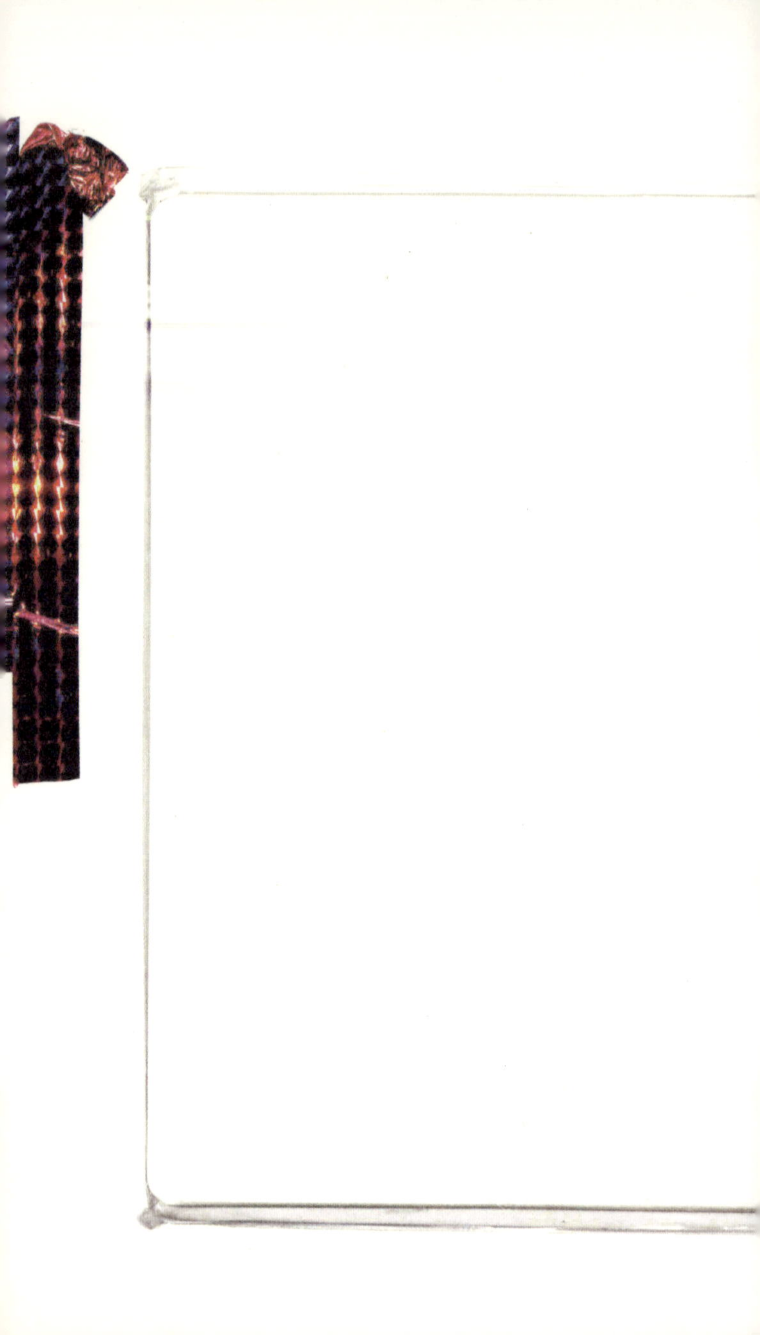

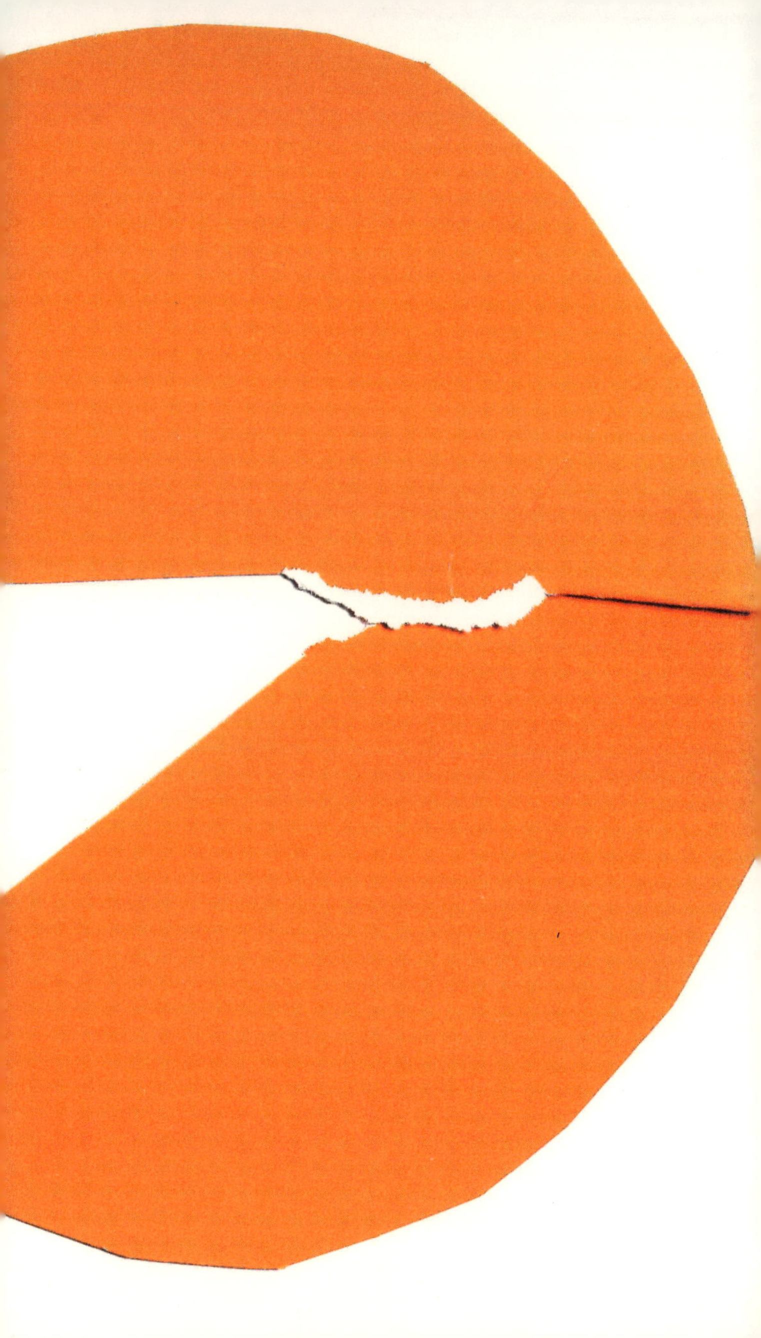

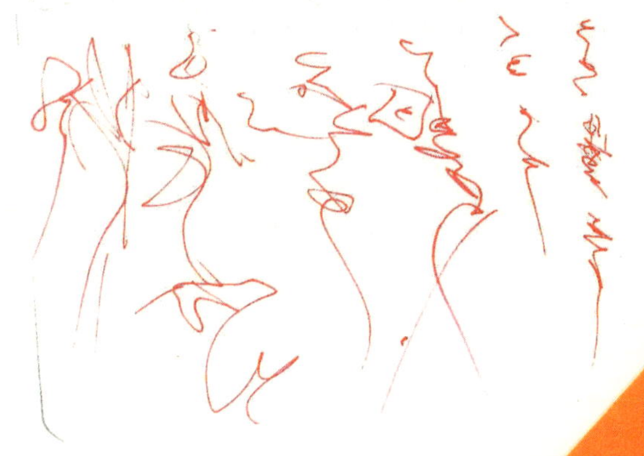

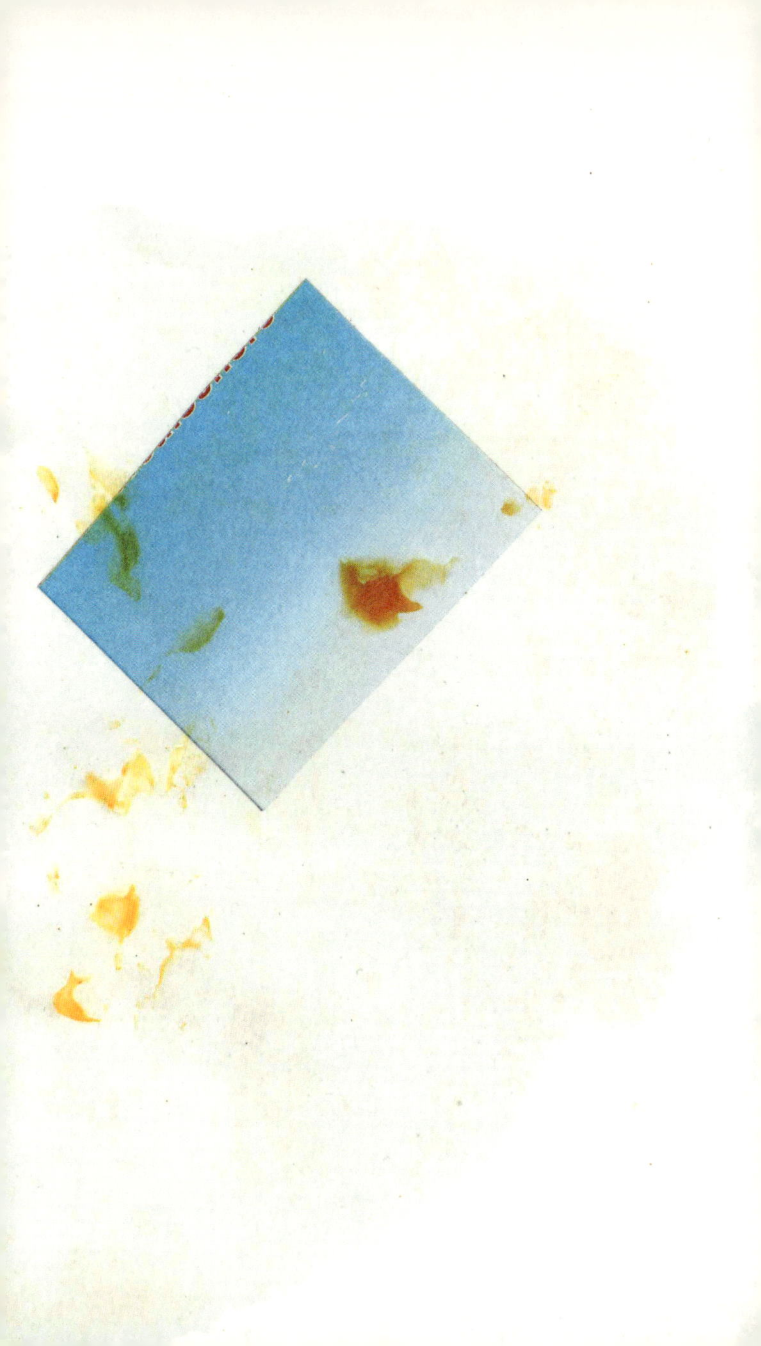

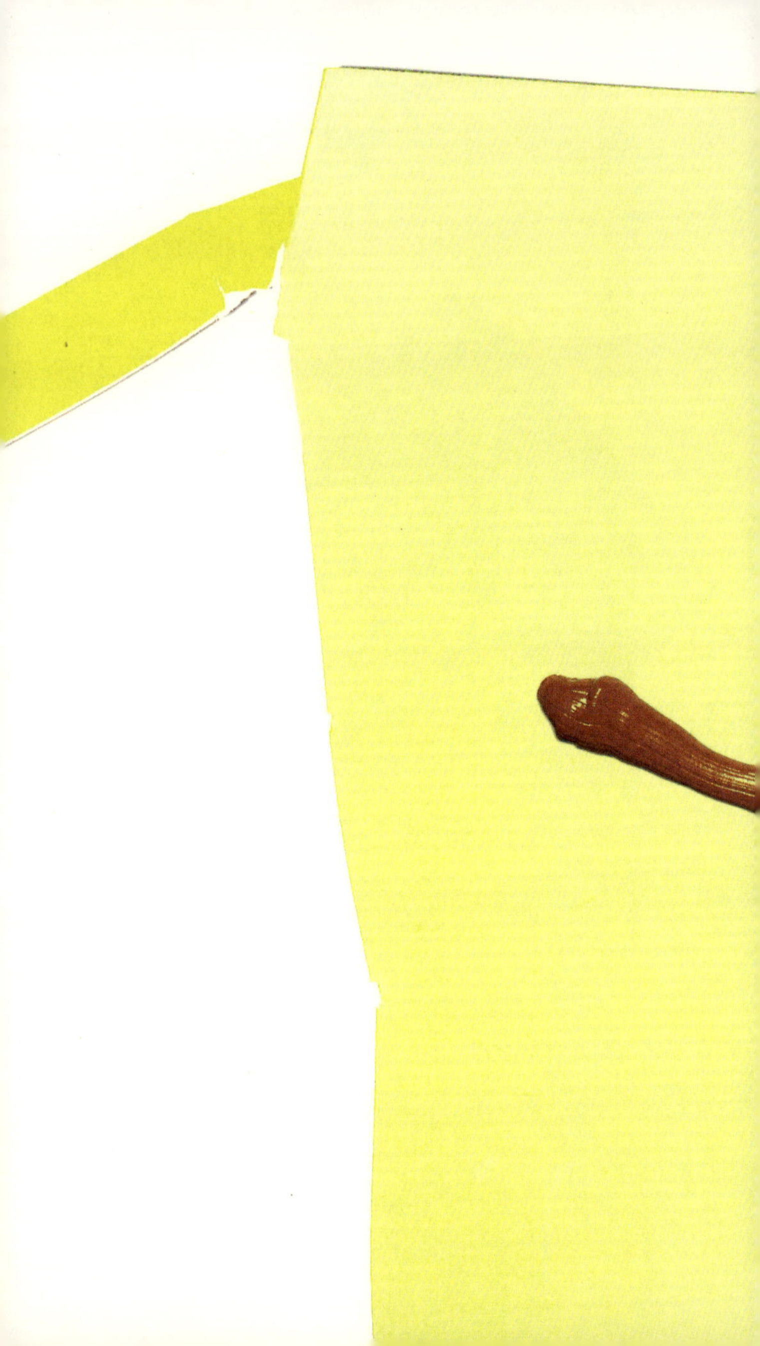

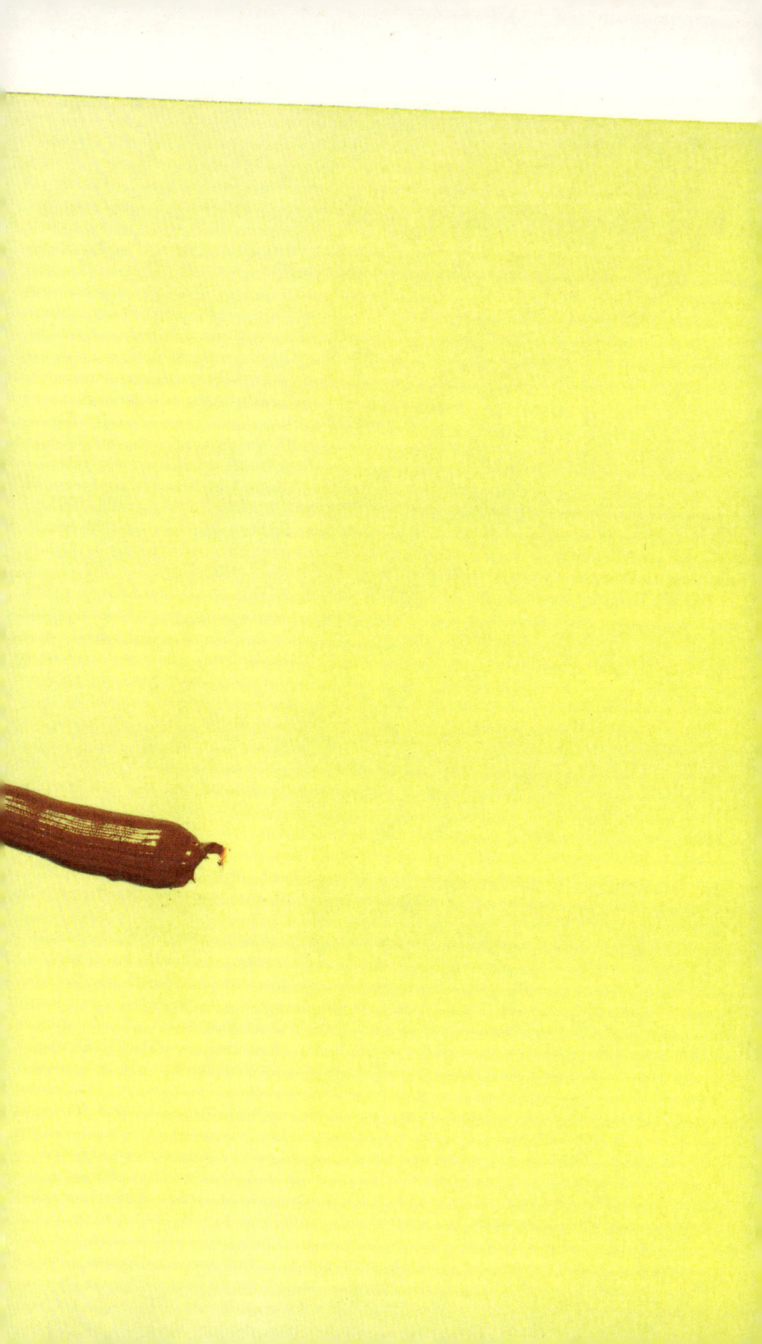

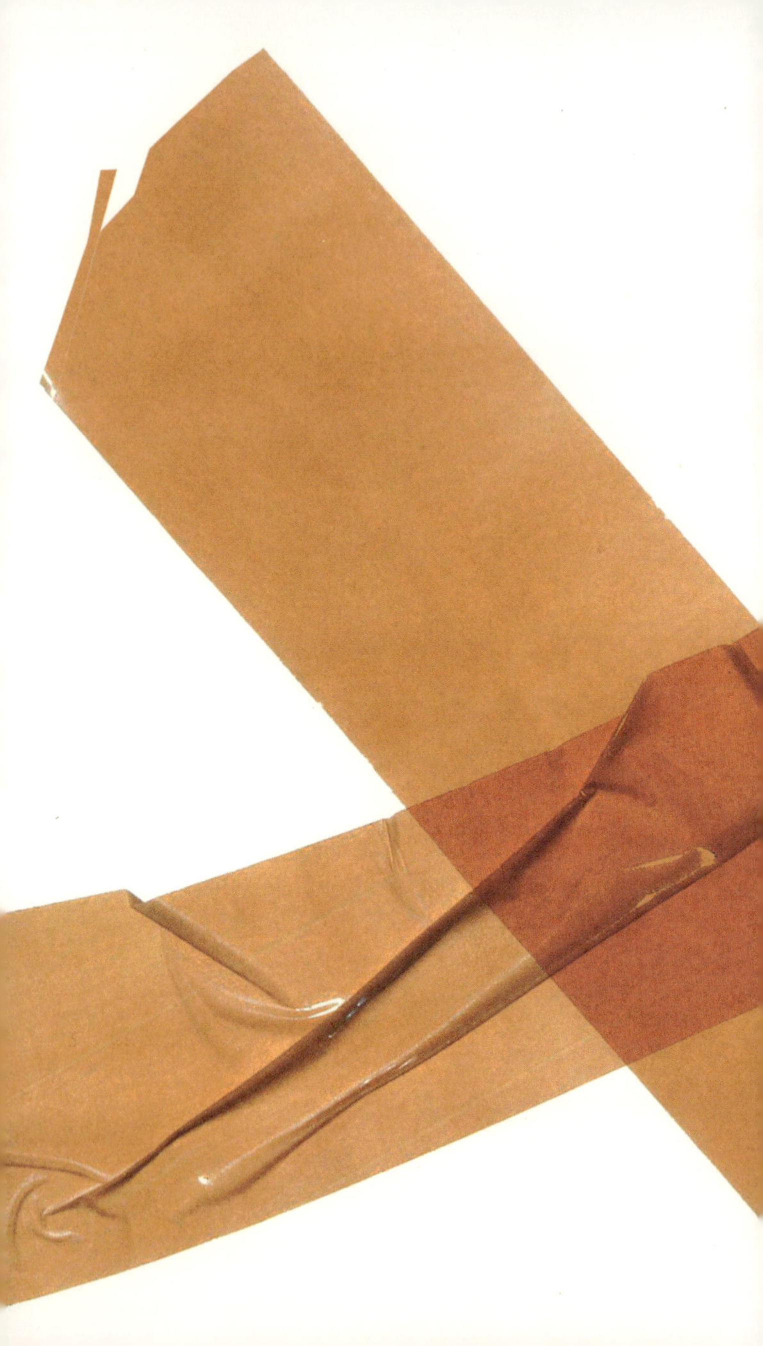

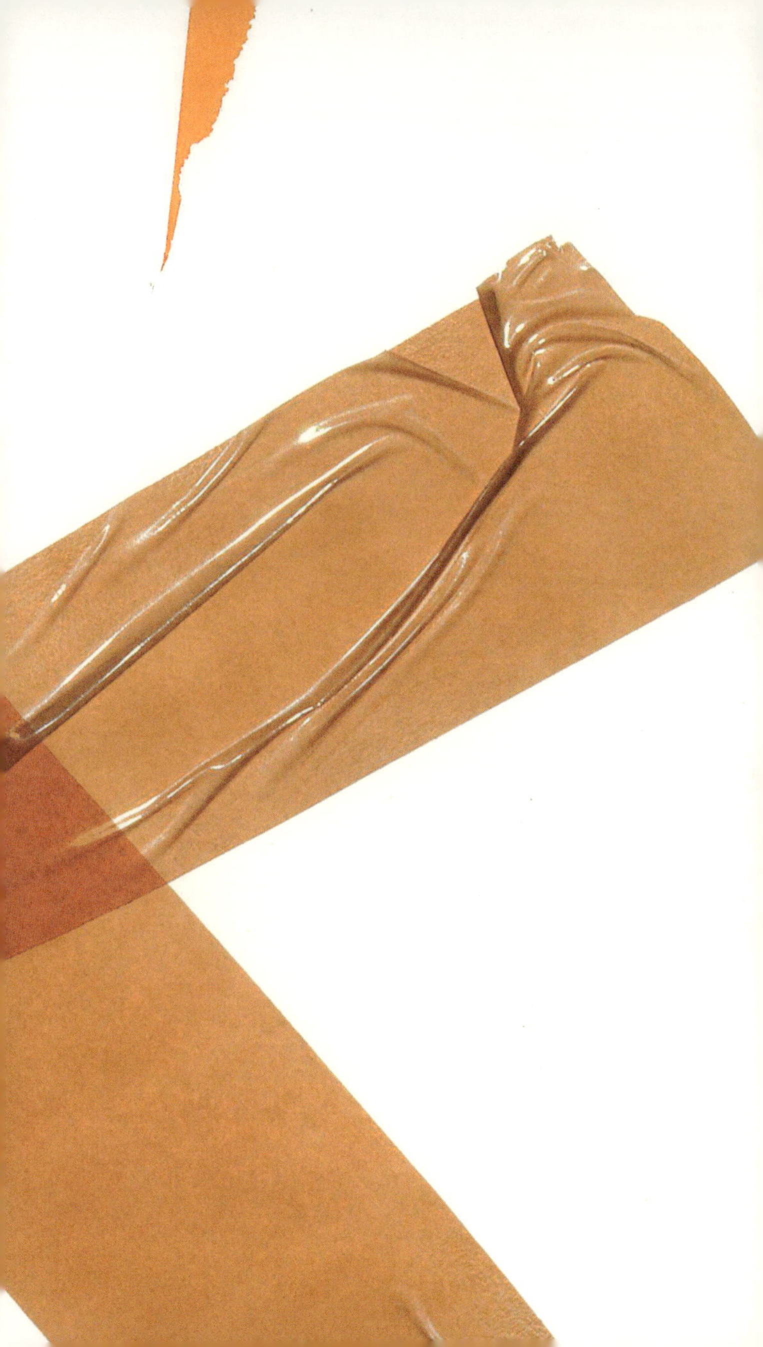

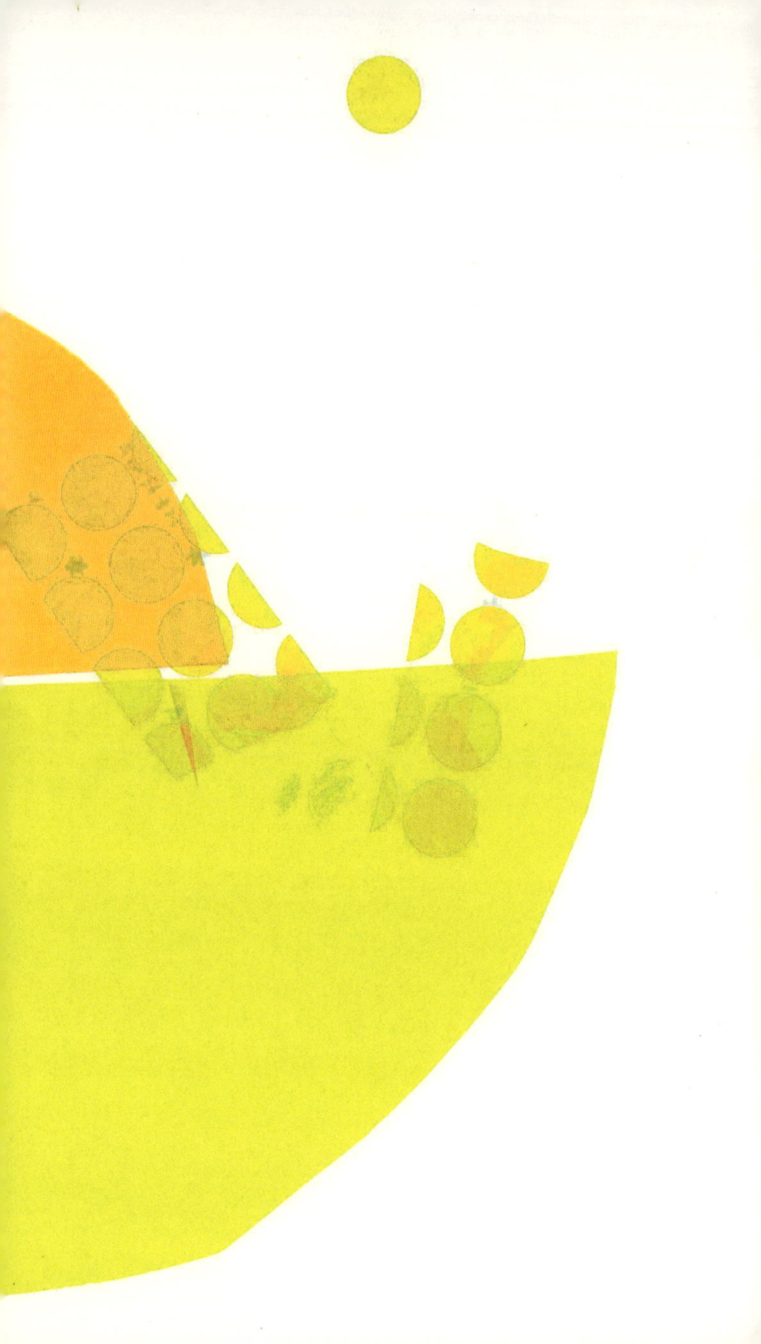

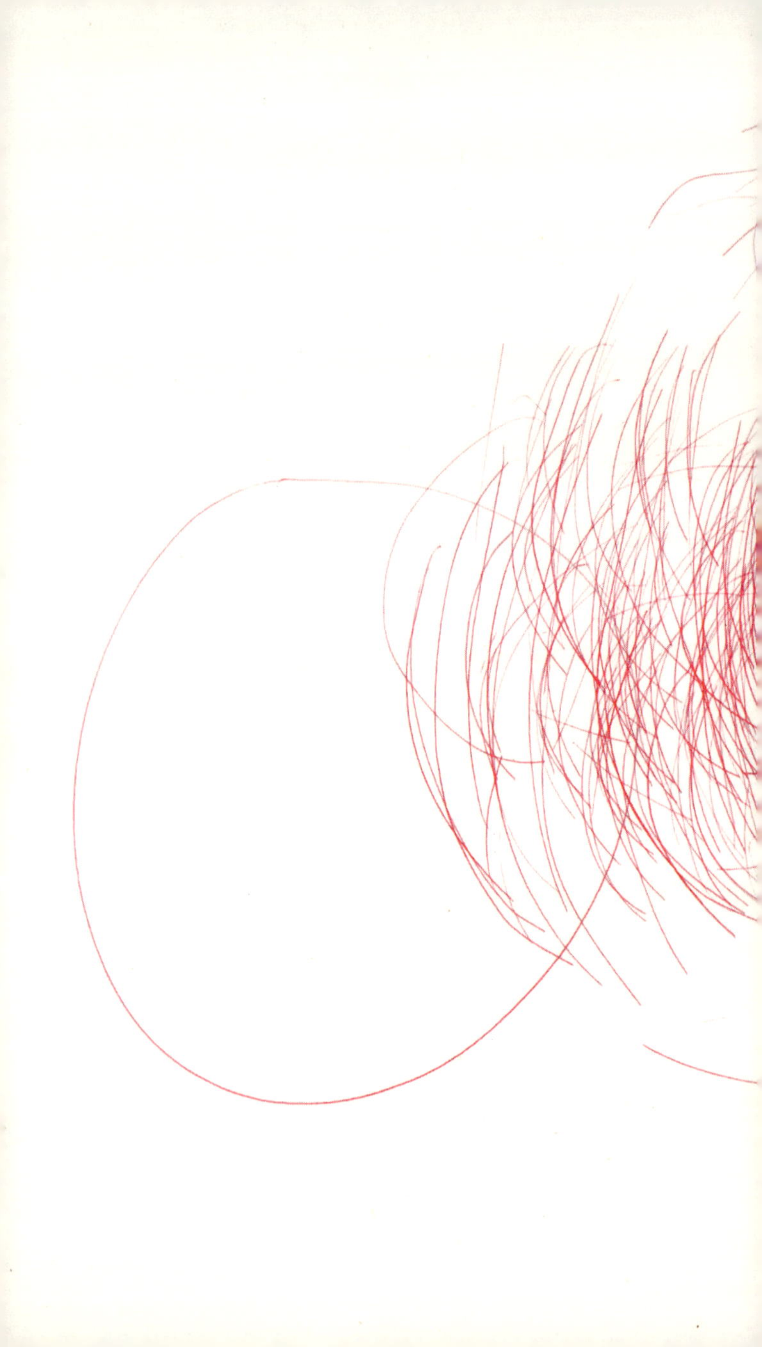

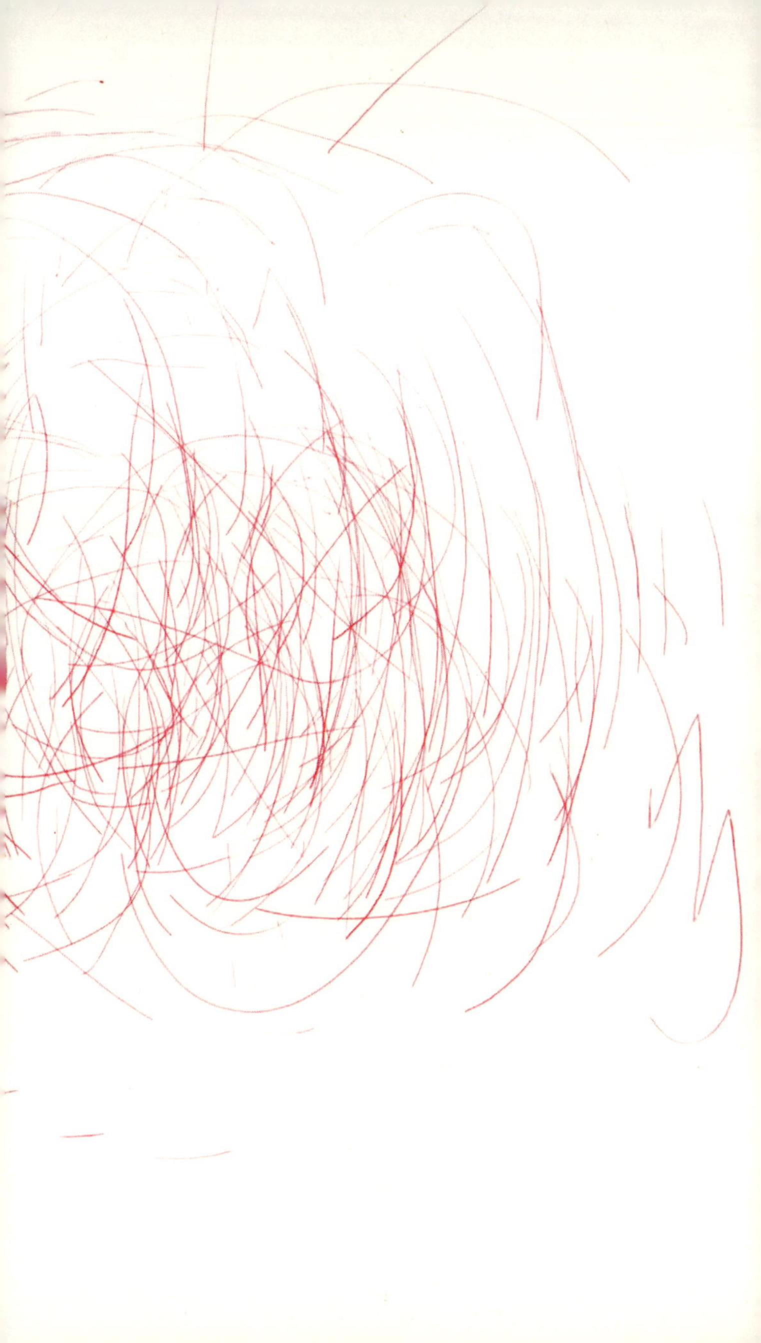

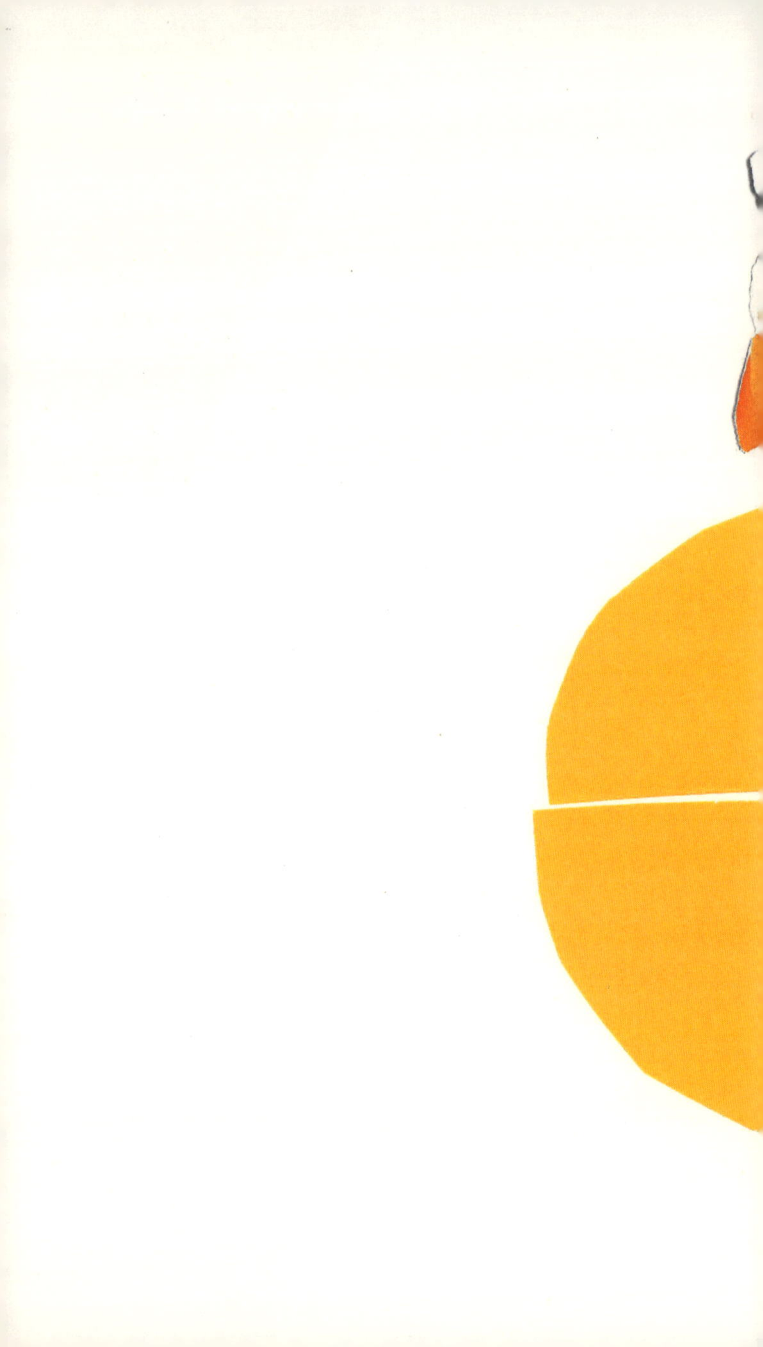

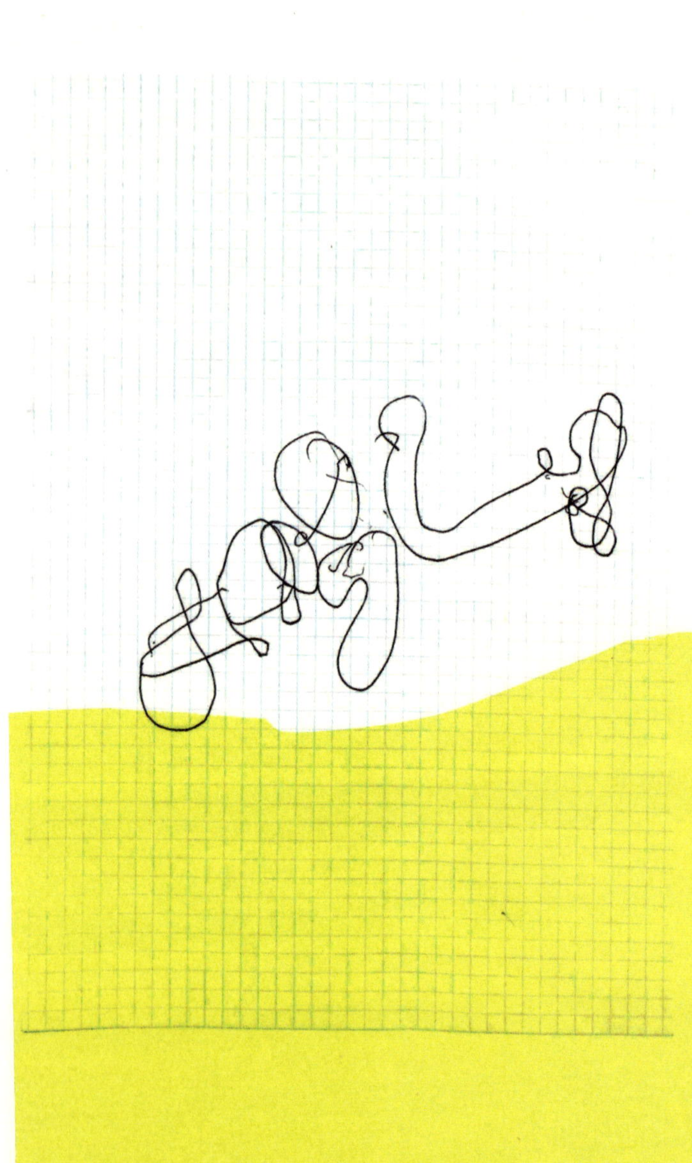

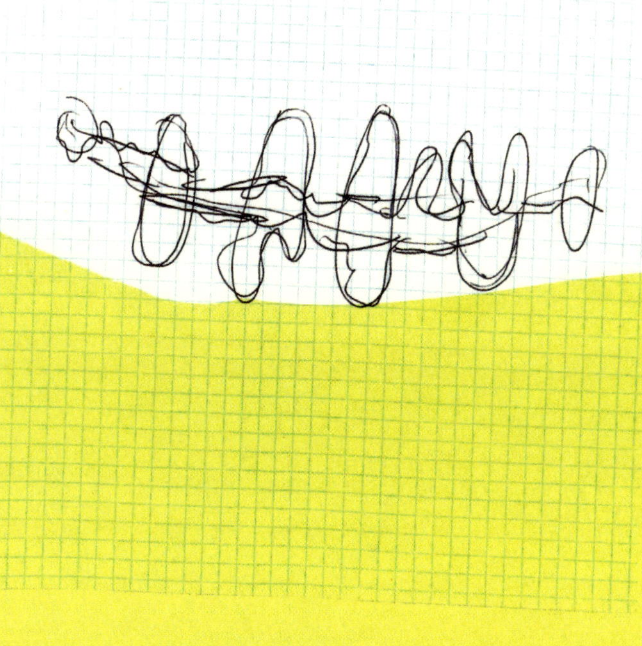

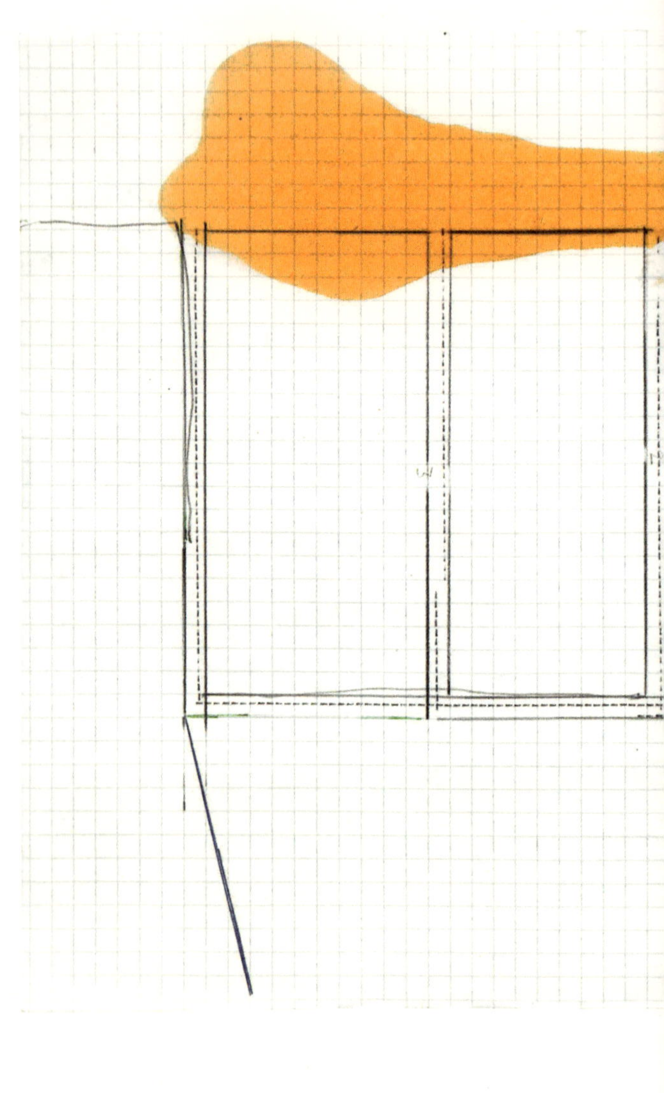

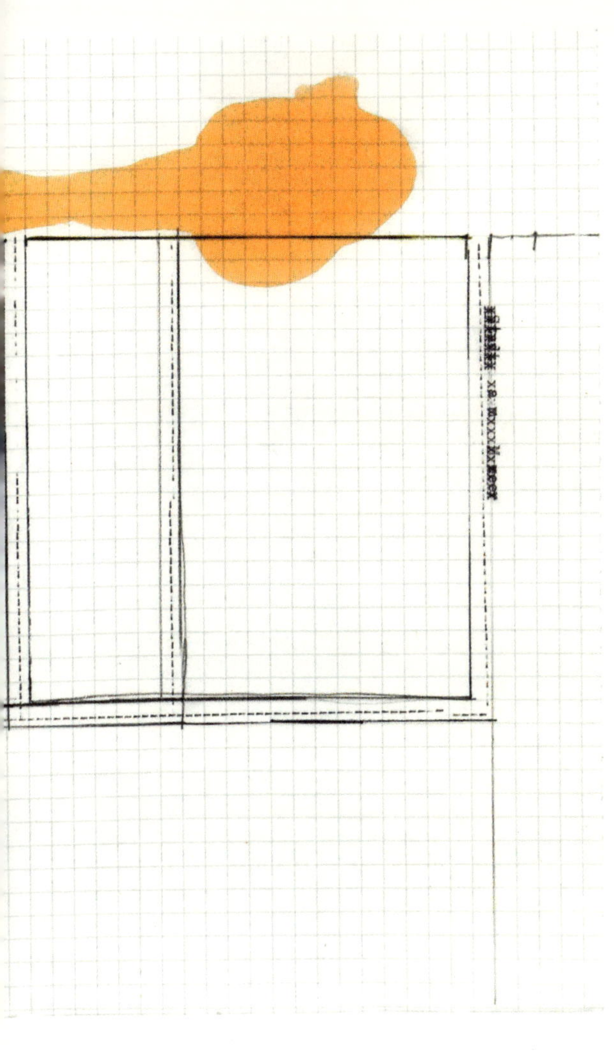

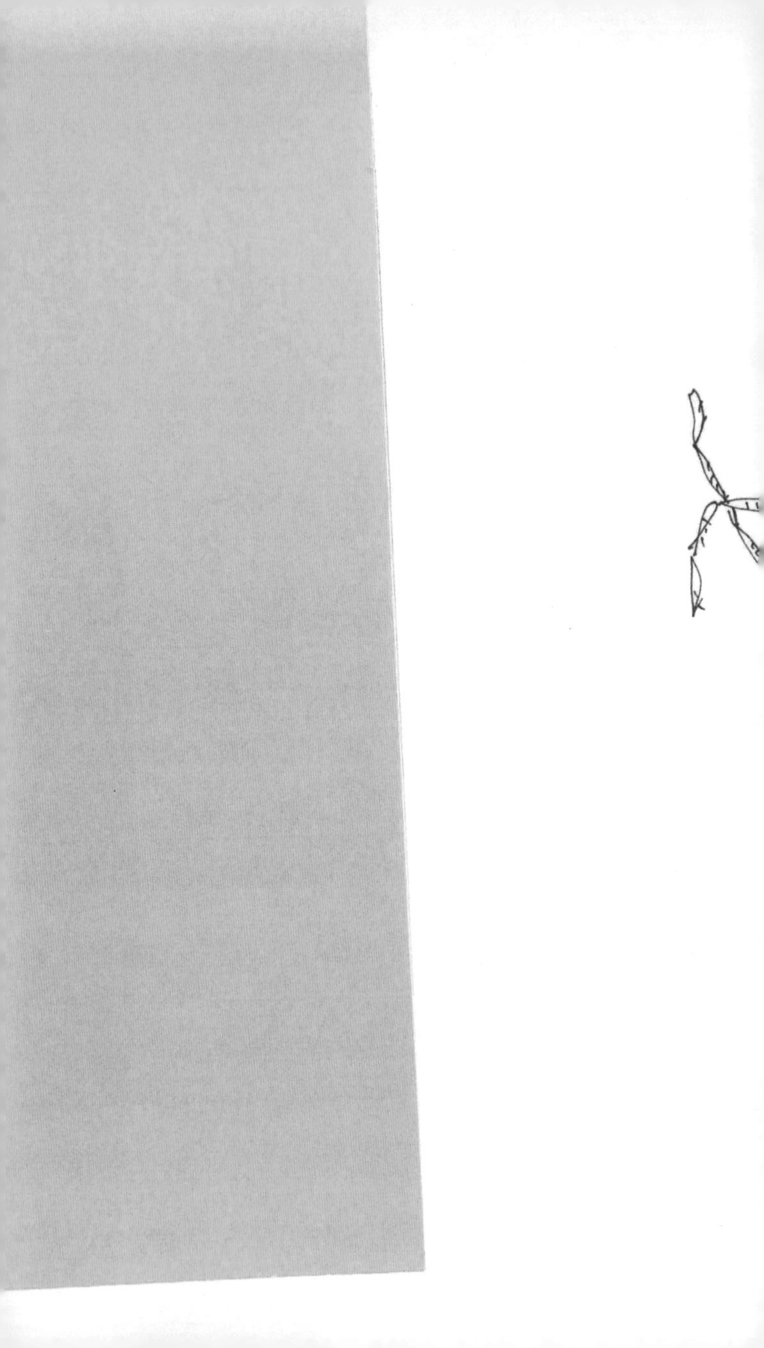

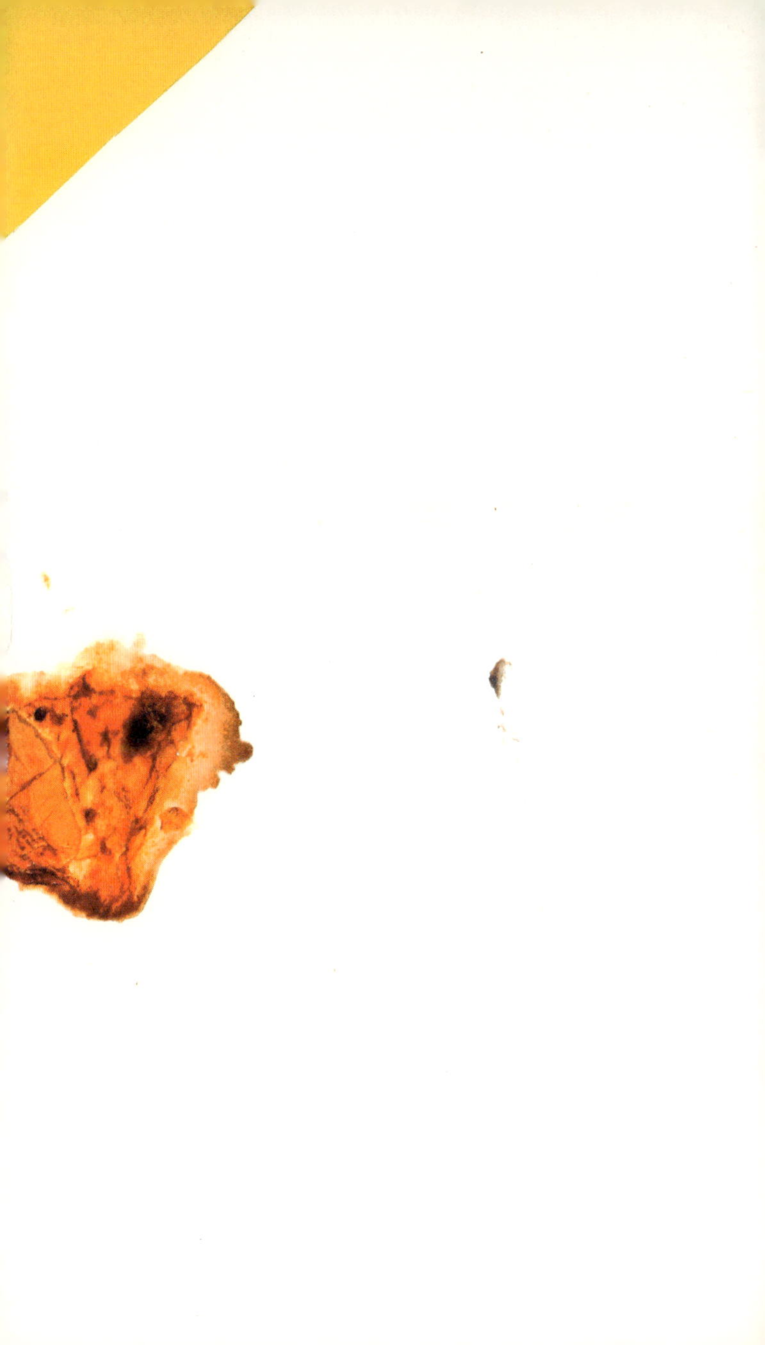

Erik Steinbrecher
Ausmalbuch

First Edition

Published by Nieves
www.nievesbooks.com

ISBN 978-3-907179-06-2